DOCTOR

IN TRAINING

←--- Can you find me
on every page?

KINGFISHER

MEDICAL ACADEMY

TRAINING PROGRAMME

DOCTOR

Ho
6/19

STUDENT PASS

Name ....

KINGFISHER

First published 2018 by Kingfisher
an imprint of Macmillan Children's Books
20 New Wharf Road, London N1 9RR
Associated companies throughout the world
www.panmacmillan.com

Series editor: Kath Jewitt
Design: Jeni Child
Consultant: Dr Patricia MacNair

ISBN 978-0-7534-4411-5

9 8 7 6 5 4 3 2 1

1TR/0119/WKT/UG/128MA

A CIP catalogue record for this book is available from the British Library.

Printed in China

Picture credits
The Publisher would like to thank the following for permission to reproduce their material.
Top = t; Bottom = b; Centre = c; Left = l; Right = r

iStock: spanteldotru (18bl), Eraxion (29tc); Science Photo Library: Power and Syred (35tl); Shutterstock: Andril Vodolazhskyi (12-13), Zimniy (18-19), Srisakorn Wonglakorn (34c), Iyla Akinshin (34-35), Suzanne Tucker (38tr).

THEORY

PRACTICAL

THEORY pages are full of important information that you need to know.

PRACTICAL pages have a task to do or a doctor skill to acquire. Tick each page when you have completed that part of your training.

THEORY 1

TRAINING TIME

So, you want to be a doctor? Are you a good listener? Can you stay calm in a crisis? Not bothered by icky stuff? Then congratulations! Your medical training starts today.

WHAT'S THE JOB?

Doctors help people to stay healthy. They know lots about the human body, and how to make poorly people better.

Every day a doctor has to...

○ See patients in the surgery or hospital, visit them at home or talk to them on the phone.

○ Give advice about how to stay healthy.

○ Carry out medical examinations.

○ Make notes about patients.

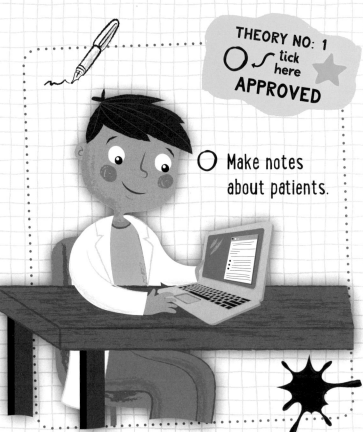

○ Write orders for medicines, called prescriptions.

MEDICAL OBSERVATION

Can you spot the patients?

Now you've got a lot to learn about the human body, so let's get started...

7

DOCTOR'S KIT

Doctors use special equipment to help them find out what is wrong with a patient. Before you begin your training, you need to collect your kit.

CHECKLIST

Can you find your kit in the surgery? Tick the box when you spot each one.

 ○ **Stethoscope** to listen to the heart and chest

 ○ **Otoscope** to look in the patient's ear

 ○ **Blood pressure monitor** to check how strong the heart is

 ○ **Sample bottle** for collecting urine (that's wee) for testing

 ○ **Penlight** to shine into dark places such as the throat

 ○ **Doctor's bag** to carry all your equipment in

BRILLIANT BODY

Your body is an amazing machine that keeps working all your life. As a doctor you'll need to know about the human body, inside and out, so prepare to discover some brilliant body facts.

BONKERS BONES

The smallest bone in the body is inside the ear. It's about the size of a grain of rice.

BITE SIZE

Children have 20 teeth and adults have 32. Baby teeth fall out and grow back as adult teeth. Enamel – the white coating on your teeth – is the hardest thing in your body.

MASSES OF MUSCLES

There are over 600 muscles in the body and 43 of them are in the face. The speediest muscle is the one that makes you blink.

WAX FACTS

Without earwax your ears would feel dry and itchy. The sticky, oily wax stops germs and dust from getting inside your ear.

BELLY BUTTON BUGS

Millions of minuscule living things, called bacteria, make their home inside your belly button.

The skin is the largest organ of your body.

RED AND RUNNY

A 10-year-old has about 2 litres of blood inside the body. That's enough to fill a really big bottle of lemonade.

HEARTY PARTY

3,000,000,000 (or 3 billion) is the number of times your heart might beat in your lifetime.

THEORY NO: 2

○ ✓ tick here

APPROVED

HAIRY SCARY

Your body is covered in millions of hairs. The only bald places are the palms of your hands, the bottoms of your feet and your lips.

HARD AS NAILS

Your nails are made from the same tough stuff as the horns of animals, such as cows and goats.

ACTIVITY

Doctors need to know your kneecaps from your elbows! Can you identify all these body parts in the big picture?

○ knee   ○ ankle   ○ wrist   ○ elbow
○ forehead   ○ jaw   ○ shoulder   ○ heel

BLOOD

Blood is a 24-hour delivery service, carrying important stuff your body needs. It travels along wiggly tubes, called blood vessels, to reach every part of your body.

Blood vessels carry blood to the brain.

Your heart is about the size of your fist.

The red tubes are called arteries.

The blue tubes are called veins.

DOCTOR'S NOTES

Delivery
The blood in the red tubes (arteries) travels from the heart around the body, ready to deliver:

food
oxygen
water
medicines
heat

Collection
The blood in the blue tubes (veins) travels back to the heart. It collects:

waste

PRACTICAL NO: 2
tick here
APPROVED

CHECKLIST

Can you find these things?

○ **Heart** – this strong muscle pumps the blood around the body.

○ **Lungs** – blood picks up an important gas here, called oxygen.

○ **Arteries** – these tubes carry blood away from the heart.

○ **Veins** – these tubes carry blood back to the heart.

○ **Capillaries** – the good stuff in blood passes through these tiny tubes to every part of the body.

○ **Liver** – blood picks up food from here.

○ **Kidneys** – blood delivers the waste stuff from the body here, where it gets cleaned up.

Can you spot the odd one out in this picture?

Take a look at what is packed into a single drop of blood.

Red blood cells: carry oxygen to every part of the body.

White blood cells: attack and destroy germs.

Platelets: make your blood sticky to stop the bleeding when you cut yourself.

Plasma: half of your blood is watery stuff that carries food and medicine around the body.

ODD ONE OUT

THE HEART

Bom-bom, bom-bom.
That's the sound of the
hard-working heart beating.
It pushes blood around your
body every second of every
single day. It can change the
amount of blood pumped
and how fast it beats.

The right side of
the heart pumps
blood to the lungs
to pick up oxygen.

Right atrium

Valv.

Right
ventricle

The heart squeezes to
pump blood around the
body. Each squeeze is
one heartbeat.

A stethoscope
makes it easier
to listen to the
heart beating.

The heart is a
powerful muscle
in the middle of
your chest.

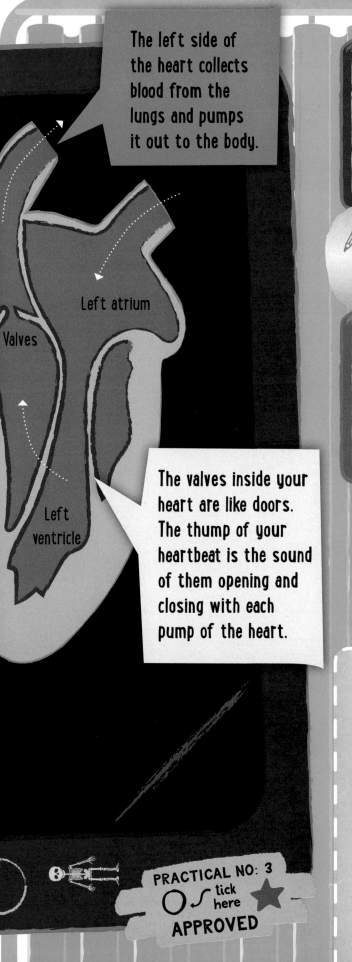

The left side of the heart collects blood from the lungs and pumps it out to the body.

Left atrium

Valves

Left ventricle

The valves inside your heart are like doors. The thump of your heartbeat is the sound of them opening and closing with each pump of the heart.

PRACTICAL NO: 3

tick here

APPROVED

SPOT THE DIFFERENCES

Heart monitor machines make a record of your heartbeat on a screen. Can you spot 6 differences between the two screens?

TAKING A PULSE

Your pulse rate is the number of times your heart beats in one minute. You can feel your pulse in your wrist because the blood flows near to the surface.

1 Hold out one hand, palm up. Press two fingers onto your wrist below the thumb until you feel thumping.

2 Use a watch to count the number of thumps in one minute.

PRACTICAL 4

BREATHING

Use your stethoscope to listen to your patient's chest as they breathe in. The lungs fill with air and give the body a boost of oxygen — the gas we need to stay alive.

BREATHE IN

1 Air travels through your mouth or nose. Hairs and snot, called mucus, trap dust and dirt and stop it getting into your lungs.

2 The air warms up as it travels down the windpipe and into the lungs.

3 Inside the lungs, air travels down lots of tubes that get smaller and branch out, just like a tree.

ACTIVITY

When you exercise, your body needs more oxygen so you breathe faster. Do 10 star jumps on the spot, then stop. Are you breathing faster now?

You breathe in and out about 20,000 times a day without even thinking about it!

4 At the end of every little tube is an air sac covered in tiny blood vessels.

5 This is where the oxygen in the air passes into the blood and is carried off around the body.

BREATHE OUT

Phew! The lungs push the waste air back up the windpipe and out through your nose or mouth.

DOCTOR'S NOTES

Coughs and sneezes

If anything blocks the air on its way to the lungs, the body gets rid of it with a cough or a sneeze.

When we cough or sneeze air shoots out of the nose and mouth, along with snot and germs. ATISHOOO! So make sure to wash your hands regularly if you have a cough or cold.

The skeleton is made of hundreds of bones, joined up to give the body its shape and protect the soft parts inside. Without bones you would be a floppy blob.

BONES

SKULL
Your skull is like a helmet, protecting the soft brain inside it.

Adult skeletons have 206 bones while babies' skeletons have 270.

SPINE
The spine has 33 bones that fit together like building blocks. Run your finger along your back. Can you feel the lumpy bones?

RIBS
Ribs protect your heart and lungs.

ELBOW
This is the elbow joint. Joints are places where two bones meet. They allow your skeleton to move.

THIGH
Your thighbone is the largest bone in the body.

Bone is living tissue. It is hard and strong, but lots of little holes inside make it light, so you can move easily.

KEEPING BONES HEALTHY

STRONG BONES
Eating food with plenty of calcium in it keeps bones healthy and strong. Calcium is special stuff found in milk and foods made from milk.

BROKEN BONES
Sometimes bones break or crack. As a doctor, you will need to check for breaks if a patient has an injury that is sore and swollen. An X-ray is a picture that shows the bones underneath the skin and muscle.

TREATMENT
Doctors sometimes wrap the broken bone in a hard plaster, called a cast, to keep it very still. Then new bone can grow to mend the break.

Can you find the broken bone in each of these X-ray pictures?

PRACTICAL NO: 5
tick here
APPROVED

1 MUSCLES TO MOVE

Long, stretchy muscles are attached to your skeleton. They pull on the bones to make them move. You are in charge so they only work when you want them to.

2 MUSCLE MAGIC

Some muscles work without you having to think about them. Right now, deep inside your body, muscles are busy mixing food in your tummy, squeezing food in your gut and squeezing the blood in your arteries to push it along.

THEORY 3

MUSCLES

Muscles make parts of your body move. Whether you are walking or sleeping, somewhere in the body, muscles are hard at work.

3 MUSCLE MARATHON

The most hard-working muscle in your body is the heart. It squeezes to pump the blood around your body at least 70 times every minute for the whole of your life.

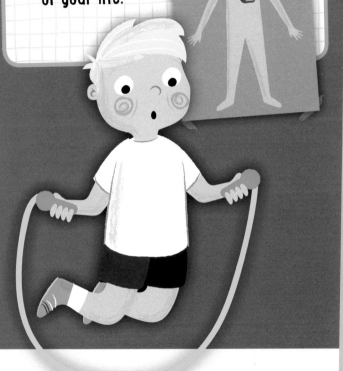

MIGHTY MUSCLES

Exercise makes your muscles bigger and stronger. Eating foods that have protein in them helps to build strong muscles too.

BEND... AND STRAIGHTEN

Bend your arm while you squeeze the top with your other hand. Can you feel the muscle bulging?

1 When you bend your arm, the muscle gets shorter.

2 When you straighten your arm, the muscle gets longer.

DOCTOR'S NOTES

What is a pulled muscle?

If you make a muscle work too hard or too fast, you might tear part of the muscle. This painful damage is called "pulling a muscle".

There are lots of fun ways to exercise your muscles. Activities such as cycling are great for strengthening your muscles.

DIGESTION

What is going on in your patient's tummy? As part of your training, you will need to know the ins and outs of the grumbly, gurgling guts.

FOOD FOR FUEL

Your body gets energy from the food that you eat. For food to turn into fuel for the body, it needs to be broken into tiny pieces. This is called digestion.

It can take up to 3 days for food to travel all the way through your body.

Saliva glands

PRACTICAL NO: 6
tick here
APPROVED

RUMBLE! RUMBLE!

Your tummy grumbles if your stomach churns when it is empty. The gases inside it make a growling sound.

CHECKLIST

Find each body part on the big picture.

○ Food is chewed in the mouth by teeth and mixed with spit, called saliva, to make it mushy.

○ Each mouthful travels down a tube called the oesophagus (say uh-sof-a-gus). Muscles in the tube push the food into the stomach.

○ The muscly walls of the stomach mix and churn the food. Strong stomach juices turn the lumps into liquid.

○ This tube is the small intestine. The good parts in the food pass through its walls and are delivered around the body.

○ The stuff left behind is waste. It travels to the large intestine. Here, water is sucked out of the leftovers and it is turned into poo.

Liver

START

EXIT

Find your way through the small intestine maze to the large intestine.

DISTANCE TRAVELLED: 8 metres

DOCTOR'S NOTES

Tummy troubles

If you eat harmful food, or catch a tummy bug, the stomach gets rid of it by sending the food back out of your mouth as vomit.

Sometimes germs or bugs get into your intestines. The body gets rid of them by making you poo more often. This is called diarrhoea (say die-o-ree-a).

23

WATERWORKS

Gulp a glass of water and before long you need a wee. But what is this watery stuff that we flush away, and how is it made? As a doctor in training, it's your job to find out!

○ Blood vessels

○ Kidney

WEE

Wee, or urine, is made up of water and other waste stuff that the body doesn't need.

1 Water from eating and drinking passes into your blood. Your blood flows through your kidneys on its journey around the body.

2 The kidneys are the body's cleaning machines. They get rid of waste and extra water as urine.

○ Bladder

3 Drip, drip – urine trickles down tubes into the bladder all day long.

4 When the bladder is full, you need to go to the toilet and the wee gushes out.

Follow each pipe to see which one has the leak.

a b c

WATER

Two thirds of your body is water, but you lose water all the time when you sweat, breathe and go to the toilet.

Your body needs at least 6 glasses of water every day to keep it topped up.

DOCTOR'S NOTES

If you drink plenty, the body makes lots of wee. If you don't drink much, the body saves water and makes a small amount of strong wee. A doctor can tell if a patient is drinking enough by the colour of their wee.

THEORY NO: 4

◯ ⤳ tick here
APPROVED

DIP TEST

Match the patient's wee with the correct colour on the chart. Has the patient drunk enough water today?

Need to drink lots of water	Drink some water	Need to drink a little water	Good! Drinking plenty

BEING HEALTHY

People need to look after their body to keep it in tip-top shape. It'll be part of your job to advise people how to stay healthy.

FAB FOOD

You need to eat lots of different foods to give your body everything it needs.

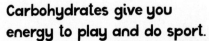

Carbohydrates give you energy to play and do sport.

Fruit and vegetables are packed with vitamins that keep your body healthy.

Find one healthy food from each group to go in your lunchbox.

Pick a healthy drink too.

DOCTOR'S NOTES

You might be asleep, but some parts of your body never rest.

- The brain dreams and keeps alert to loud noises.
- Skin mends cuts and bruises.
- The heart keeps beating.
- The lungs keep breathing air.
- The stomach and intestines digest food.
- The kidneys keep making urine.
- Bones keep growing.

THEORY NO: 5
tick here
APPROVED

Fat gives you a store of energy, but you only need a small amount of it.

Protein helps your body to grow and mend itself.

SUPER SLEEP

Sleeping gives your body a chance to rest and repair itself.

Babies need lots of sleep. 15 to 20 hours altogether!

GROWING

The body needs more sleep when it is young and still growing.

ZZZZZZ

Young children need 10 to 12 hours' sleep.

DREAMS

You dream every night, but you might not always remember your dreams. Can you remember what you dreamed about last night?

Teenagers need 8 to 10 hours' sleep.

Grown-ups need about 8 hours' sleep.

sneezing and coughing

swollen itchy eyes

SYMPTOMS

Allergies make people feel unwell in different ways.

- runny nose
- sneezing
- swollen itchy eyes
- coughing
- wheezy chest
- sickness
- upset tummy
- itchy rashes

itchy rashes

PRACTICAL 7

ALLERGIES

An allergy is when something that is normally harmless makes you feel ill. For the next part of your training, head for the park to spot all the things that can cause allergies.

UNDER THE MICROSCOPE

Dust mites are very tiny creatures that live in every home. You can't see them or feel them, but some people are allergic to their teeny poos.

wheezy chest

upset tummy

sickness

runny nose

How many bees are in the picture?

CHECKLIST

Can you find all of the different things that cause allergies?

 ○ **Nuts**, such as hazelnuts, almonds and peanuts

 ○ **Pollen** – the dust made by flowers that floats in the air

 ○ **Insect stings**, especially wasp and bee stings

 ○ **Fish** and **shellfish**, such as prawns

 ○ **Wheat**, found in bread, biscuits and cake

 ○ **Milk** and foods made from milk

 ○ **Fur** from animals

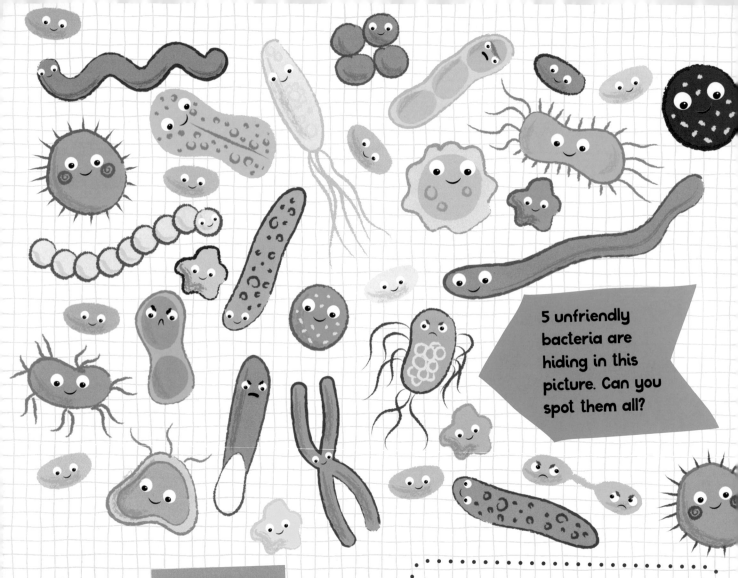

5 unfriendly bacteria are hiding in this picture. Can you spot them all?

BATTLING BUGS

We are surrounded by millions of tiny living things called bacteria. These are found just about everywhere on our planet. Some are good and some are bad, so it's a doctor's job to help people keep the bad ones away.

GOODIES AND BADDIES

Lots of bacteria are harmless, and many are good for us. Your stomach and intestines are full of friendly bacteria that help you to digest your food and fight off illness.

Some kinds of bacteria can make you unwell if they get inside your body. We call them germs.

WHERE DO GERMS LIVE?

○ On your hands and things that have been touched by lots of other people's hands.

○ On old or mouldy food and raw meat.

○ On the soles of your shoes and on the pavements and ground where they walk.

○ Coughs and sneezes are full of germs.

KEEP THEM OUT!

Your body has lots of clever ways of keeping out germs.

1 **Nose**: germs in the air that you breathe get caught by tiny hairs and slimy snot (called mucus).

2 **Eye**: tears wash away germs.

3 **Ears**: earwax slowly flows out of your ears, taking germs and dirt with it.

4 **Skin**: this protective cover all over your body helps stop germs getting inside.

1

2

3

4

DOCTOR'S NOTES

How to protect against germs:

Wash your hands after going to the loo, touching anything dirty, and before you eat.

Cover your mouth and nose when you cough or sneeze, then wash your hands.

THEORY NO: 6
○ tick here
APPROVED

MEDICINES

Our body is good at looking after itself, but sometimes we need help to get better, or to keep us safe from diseases. As a trainee doctor, it's time for you to get the low-down on medicines.

! DOCTOR'S WARNING

BE SAFE WITH MEDICINES!

1. Never take a medicine that is not for you – it could make you really ill.

2. Never take more than it says you need.

3. Grown-ups are in charge of giving medicines.

If patients are unwell they might need medicine to help them feel better.

VACCINATIONS

A tiny amount of the germ that causes the illness is injected into the body. It's not enough to make you ill, but the body learns to fight the germ, protecting you from it in the future.

Can you spot the odd one out in the bottles above?

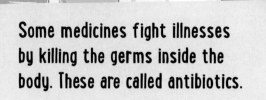

Some medicines fight illnesses by killing the germs inside the body. These are called antibiotics.

Some medicines soothe pain, such as from an earache or a sore throat. They can't make you well, but they make you feel better while you are recovering.

People with asthma find it hard to breathe. They use an inhaler with medicine inside to open up the breathing tubes and help them to breathe more easily.

Some medicines cannot be swallowed, so they have to be injected instead.

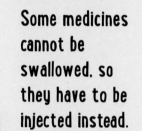

PRESCRIPTIONS

Can you find these medicines on the shelves:

O Cough medicine

O Skin rash cream

O Eye drops

PRACTICAL NO: 8
O ↙ tick here
APPROVED

SKIN

Your skin is a stretchy covering that wraps around your whole body. It may seem smooth and unexciting, but take a closer look – there's important stuff happening just under the surface!

WATERPROOFING

The top layer of skin is waterproof. That's why you don't fill up with water when you have a bath or go swimming.

SUN PROTECTION

The skin stops your insides from drying out in the sun's heat. It also has protective stuff in it, called melanin, which stops your skin from burning.

○ People with lots of melanin have darker skin.

○ Freckles and moles are small patches of skin with lots of melanin.

! DOCTOR'S WARNING!

Sun safety
Too much sunshine can damage skin. All patients should:

1. Put on plenty of sun cream.
2. Cover up with a hat and a T-shirt.
3. Stay in the shade during the hottest time of the day.

GERM CONTROL

Skin helps to stop dirt and germs from getting inside your body so look after your skin!

FLAKY STUFF

Thousands and thousands of flakes of dead skin fall off your body every minute.

SKIN SPOT

Look closely at your skin. Tick the box for each of these that you spot:

○ freckle   ○ hair
○ mole   ○ sweat pore

HAIRY

The hairs on your skin stand up when you are cold. This traps a layer of air to keep you warm.

HEATING

A layer of fat under your skin acts like a blanket to keep you warm.

This is a picture of what is under your skin.

○ Hair   ○ Pore

○ Fat layer   ○ Sensor

COOLING

Sweat comes out of tiny holes called pores. When sweat dries on your skin it cools you down.

FEELING

Sensors in your skin tell you when you touch something hot or cold, wet or dry, smooth or sharp.

THEORY 8

CUTS AND BRUISES

Bumps, cuts and scrapes are all part of life for your skin. Luckily, it is very good at repairing itself. Before you can even reach for your doctor's bag, the body is already on the case.

ACTIVITY

Can you spot...

○ a blister

○ a cut finger

○ a bruise

on these pages?

When you cut your skin, blood spills out. Special blood cells, called platelets, leap into action to plug the hole. They make your blood thick and sticky. This is called clotting.

HEALING HOLES

Platelets arrive at the cut.

The platelets clot to make a plug.

The plug hardens into a scab.

The scab falls off, leaving new skin.

When you bump yourself, tiny blood vessels break and blood leaks out underneath your skin. This is called a bruise. The bruise goes through some colourful changes as it heals.

LUMPS AND BUMPS

DAY 1

DAY 3

DAY 5

DAY 7

A blister is a round bubble of clear liquid under the skin. Blisters form when the skin is rubbed, so you might get one on your heel if your shoe rubs, or on your hand from holding a racket to hit a ball.

DOCTOR'S NOTES

DO put a plaster on a cut or blister to keep it clean until it starts to heal.

DON'T pick scabs or pop blisters! You could let germs get under the skin.

BLISTERS

A blister can be painful, but it is a squishy cushion that protects the area underneath from more damage.

THEORY NO: 8

tick here

APPROVED

A scanning machine shows a picture of the unborn baby on a screen.

Being a doctor means looking after everybody, from tiny babies and young children to grown-ups and old people. Doctors even look after babies before they are born!

PRACTICAL 9

GROWING

From the moment a baby is born, its body is growing and its brain is learning. Match each picture with the right description.

○ Bella spends time with friends. She can do a lot of things on her own – and she's growing very fast.

80 YEARS OLD

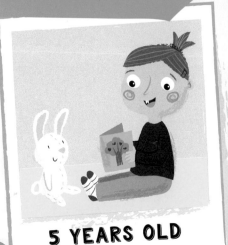

5 YEARS OLD

○ Bella cries, feeds and sleeps for most of the day.

25 YEARS OLD

BABIES

It's hard to believe that a baby starts life as a tiny speck, smaller than a pinhead.

The father's sperm joins with the mother's egg and the baby begins to grow in the mother's womb.

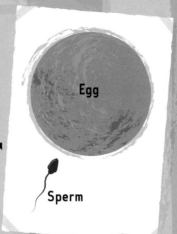

Egg

Sperm

GETTING BIGGER

The baby changes every week as it grows inside the mother. It takes 9 months, or about 40 weeks, before the baby is ready to be born.

1 month

3 months

6 months

9 months

○ Bella has wrinkled skin and grey hair. She needs to wear glasses.

NEWBORN

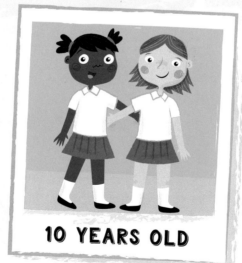

10 YEARS OLD

○ Bella has reached her full size. She can have babies of her own.

○ Bella has lost some of her baby teeth now, and big ones are starting to grow. She is learning to read, write and do sums.

Measure how tall you are. Then keep a record and see how much you grow during 1 year.

Everyone looks different, but families share a lot of the same features, such as hair colour. This is because parents pass on their genes to their children.

PRACTICAL 10

FAMILIES

The waiting room is packed with families waiting to see the doctor! Can you help the receptionist match up the children with their parents?

CHECKLIST

The genes you get from your parents control lots of things about the way you are. Look at the things in this list. Tick the features you share with other members of your family.

- ◯ eye colour
- ◯ hair colour
- ◯ left or right handed
- ◯ straight hair
- ◯ curly hair
- ◯ freckles
- ◯ nose shape

Genes are like a set of instructions that make you the way you are. Children get some of their genes from their father and some from their mother.

Brothers and sisters often look similar because they share a lot of the same genes.

Identical twins look the same because nearly all their genes are the same.

HIPPOCRATES

Hippocrates was a doctor in Ancient Greece. His ideas about medicine and disease were so exciting and new that he is still known as the "father of medicine" today.

WILHELM RONTGEN

Wilhelm discovered how to take pictures that showed the bones inside the body. This made it much easier to repair breaks. He called the pictures X-rays.

ELIZABETH GARRETT ANDERSON

Elizabeth Garrett Anderson was the first woman to qualify as a doctor in the UK. She worked hard to provide medical care for women and children, and set up the first hospital to be staffed by women.

EDWARD JENNER

Edward Jenner was the first doctor to vaccinate people against a disease called smallpox. The vaccination saved thousands of lives and smallpox was beaten. Thanks to him there are now vaccinations for lots of diseases.

HALL OF FAME

ELIZABETH BLACKWELL

Elizabeth was the first modern-day woman to go to university and become a doctor of medicine in the US. She opened The Medical College for Women, so other women could train to be doctors and surgeons too.

ALEXANDER FLEMING

Fleming discovered the first antibiotic when he noticed that mould growing on one of his germ specimens had killed the bacteria. Antibiotics have saved millions of lives since then.

WILLIAM T.G. MORTON

People used to have operations without anything to take away the pain. William T.G. Morton was the first person to use an anaesthetic, making operations painless for the first time.

JANE WRIGHT

Jane Wright was a brilliant doctor and surgeon who worked in medical research, developing new and better ways to treat different kinds of cancer.

These people have all played a part in saving lives and beating disease with their important work.

Now it's time to see how much you have learned.

1 What is the name of the paper that has a patient's medicine written on it?
a) description
b) prescription
c) preschool

2 What tool does a doctor use to listen to a patient's heart?
a) kaleidoscope
b) telescope
c) stethoscope

3 Which of these things would you not find on your skin?
a) freckles
b) moles
c) voles

4 What is the name of the special gas that your body needs?
a) oxygen
b) oxen
c) smidgen

5 What is the name for the number of beats that the heart makes in a minute?
a) the drum
b) the pump
c) the pulse rate

6 What do you need to mend a broken bone?
a) a mast
b) a cast
c) a fast

7 What are all the bones in your body called?
a) structure
b) plankton
c) skeleton

8 Which of these is a muscle?
a) the heart
b) the brain
c) the nose

9 What is digestion?

   a) a very blocked nose

   b) blockages caused by food
     in the body

   c) how your body turns food
     into energy

10 Which of these body parts does
NOT break down food?

   a) the stomach

   b) the lungs

   c) the small intestine

11 How many glasses of water do you
need to drink each day?

   a) 6

   b) 16

   c) 1

12 What is the proper word for
"wee"?

   a) latrine

   b) urine

   c) marine

13 Which sorts of foods should
we eat more of?

   a) sweet and sticky

   b) fresh and fruity

   c) fried and salty

14 What is a vaccination?

   a) an examination by the doctor

   b) a test to see if you have
     caught an illness

   c) something that stops you
     catching an illness

MEDICAL SCORES

Check your answers at the back of the book and add up your score.

1 to 5 Oops! Get back to the surgery and swat up on your body facts.

6 to 10 You are well on your way to becoming a top doctor.

11 to 14 Top of the class! You really know your stuff, doc!

DOCTOR SPEAK

antibiotic
A medicine that kills harmful germs in the body.

bacteria
Tiny living things, some of which cause diseases.

blood vessels
The tubes that carry blood around the body.

calcium
White, chalky stuff that is found in teeth and bones.
It is also found in milk and foods made from milk.

carbohydrates
Stuff found in foods, such as bread and pasta, that gives
you energy.

digestion
Breaking down the food you eat into energy for your body.

oxygen
The gas in the air that plants and animals need to live.

platelet
A kind of blood cell in the body that stops bleeding.

prescription
A note from a doctor to a chemist saying which medicines a
patient needs.

protein
Stuff found in food and drink, such as meat, eggs and milk, that you need to grow and be healthy.

stethoscope
A tool that a doctor uses to listen to your heart and breathing.

vomit
Food and drink that comes back up from the stomach and out of the mouth.

womb
The place inside a woman's body where a baby grows before it is born.

MEDICAL ACADEMY

WELL DONE!

You made it through your doctor training.

Name...

DOCTOR

FULLY QUALIFIED

ANSWERS

Page 6
The things to find are circled below.

Page 8
The things to find are circled below.

Page 10
The things to find are circled to the side.

Page 13
The odd one out is circled below.

The things to find are circled below.

Page 15
The six differences are circled to the side.

Page 19
The broken bones are circled below.

Page 23
The things to find are circled to the side.

Page 23 (bottom)
The path through the maze is shown below.

Page 25
Pipe c has the leak.

Page 29
The things that cause allergies are circled below.

There are 4 bees.

Pages 30–31
The things to find are circled below.

Pages 32–33
The medicines are circled below.

The odd one out is circled to the side.

Pages 36–37
The things to find are circled below.

Pages 38–39
The correct matches are below.

 Newborn. Bella cries, feeds and sleeps for most of the day.

 25 years old. Bella has reached her full size.

 5 years old. Bella has lost some of her baby teeth.

 80 years old. Bella has wrinkled skin and grey hair.

 10 years old. Bella spends time with friends.

Pages 38–39
Parents and their children are the same coloured circle below.

Pages 44–45
1=b; 2=c; 3=c; 4=a; 5=c; 6=b= 7=c;
8=a; 9=c; 10=b; 11=a; 12=b; 13=b; 14=c.